SUFFERING, SILENCE, PRAYER
Ways to God

GEORGE BANN, O.S.B. (Oblate)

Suffering, Silence, Prayer

Ways to God

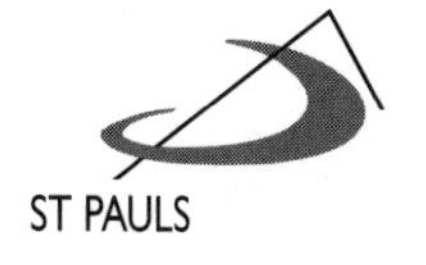

ACKNOWLEDGEMENTS
The author and publishers are obliged to the following:
The Division of Christian Education of the national Council of Churches for quotations from the R.S.V. Bible. The Cambridge University Press for quotations from the R.V. Bible and the King James Version. The Delegates of the Oxford University Press and The Syndics of the Cambridge University Press for quotations from the New English Bible. Collins Liturgical Publications for quotations from The Psalms – A new translation for worship. Editions du Centurion for permission to translate from *l'Humilité de Dieu* by François Varillon, SJ. Editions Desclée de Brouwer for permission to translate from *Le Silence de la Prière* by Dom Georges Lefebvre.

Whilst every effort has been made to contact the copyright holders of extracts used in this book, this has not always been successful. Full acknowledgement will gladly be made in future editions.

ST PAULS Publishing
187 Battersea Bridge Road, London SW11 3AS, UK
www.stpauls.ie

ISBN 085439 673 X

Set by TuKan DTP, Fareham, UK
Printed by Interprint Ltd, Marsa, Malta

ST PAULS is an activity of the priests and brothers
of the Society of St Paul who proclaim the Gospel
through the media of social communication

CONTENTS

Introduction

In the pages that follow, the thoughts expressed on the theme of "suffering, silence, prayer" are not simply the fruit of speculative research. They represent above all a personal testimony of actual experience gained in the course of a lifetime. It must be conceded that personal experience as such is incommunicable. But if the author has recorded it in writing, it is because the object he has in mind is to convey a message of peace and hope, even if only one person in distress receives that message.

However, as we consider the trilogy "suffering, silence, prayer", does the author not give us the feeling that we are being drawn into an introspective thought process, into a dialectic at three levels of wisdom: philosophical, theological and mystical? May it not be inferred from his reasoning that he has found the course of spiritual progress on three pathways that are traditionally designated as purgative, illuminative and unitive?

Suffering is a question that has always troubled the minds of men and women: we seek an answer to it with our own reason. But it has to be acknowledged that the problem of evil is insoluble from a philosophical standpoint; one should be somewhat wary of systems that provide explanations either of an optimistic character (evil would be the shadow of good, considered as integrated in the total harmony of the world) or of a pessimistic character (evil would be inherent in the sinful created human being). In reality, the only metaphysical answer to the question is of an existential order, as Pope John Paul II has pointed out: "Suffering appears to belong to the transcendency of man: this is one of the points on which man is in a sense "destined" to surpass himself, and he is called to do so in a mysterious way" (Apostolic Letter on suffering, No 5). Suffering is an occasion for man to advance in maturity on a path of drastic purification. Fr Varillon explains this: "Suffering is a mystery of purgatory. The living God is nothing but love, and if my calling as a man to come into this life is to be fulfilled, I must be made capable of loving as he loves, without retiring within myself... Suffering is dying to self in order to be purified of all egoism."

Silence, to which rational man is reduced, accordingly makes it possible to leave the word to God: it is at this theological level that the Revelation brings true light. But the light shines as if in the gloom of night. Suffering has in fact reached its climax in the passion of Christ. On the Cross, Jesus cries out to his Father: "My God, why hast thou forsaken me?" The answer is, that the Father so loved the world that he gave his only Son, that everyone who believes in him should have eternal life. The Cross reveals the love of the Father, who is wounded to the heart by the misery of men. "The supreme good of the Redemption of the world has been drawn from the Cross of Christ and continually finds its starting point in the Cross. Love creates good by drawing it from evil by means of suffering joined to love" (JP II No 18 passim). The silence of God is a measure of his humility.

Prayer, as considered on the plane of mystical wisdom, is thus the pathway to union with God. By virtue of prayer, man is made worthy to be associated with the Creator and to participate in the divine government. The sole request to be made in order to experience this efficacy is that of the "Our Father": "Your will be done." This is precisely what that sorely tried person who inspired this little book had so well understood when she wrote: "The best thing is to ask God to lead us on *his* road, to have great confidence in him, knowing that he will be with us." The author picks up and develops this central theme, bringing the reader to a general conclusion which in fact points the same way: "If we are self-effacing before the Lord in an act of humility and deep faith in the immense mystery of Love in which we are enwrapped, he will then come forward and reach out to support us and comfort us."

In order to illustrate this triad – *suffering, silence, prayer* – it is helpful to quote the address given by Pope John Paul II to an audience of sick and suffering persons on 15 August, 1983. The following passage is significant:

"I should like to leave in your memories and in your hearts three small shining lights which seem to me to be precious:

– In the first place, whatever form your suffering takes, whether physical or moral, personal or relating to your family, apostolic or otherwise connected with the Church, it is important that you should take notice and consider the problem with a lucid mind, without either minimising or overestimating the degree of suffering and all the accompanying disturbances produced in your human sensitivity: failure, uselessness of your life, and so on.

– As a second step, it is essential to advance on the road to acceptance: Yes, to accept that this is the way things are, not with more or less blind resignation but because faith gives us the assurance that the Lord is able to and desires to draw good from evil. How many of us would be able to bear witness to the fact that an ordeal accepted in faith has given them a renewed sense of serenity, hope... the love of life as a gift of God...?

– Finally, the most noble gesture remains to be made: that of oblation. The offering of one's person which is made by love for the Lord and for our brothers enables one to attain what can sometimes be a very high degree of 'theologal' charity, that is to say to become rapt in the love of Christ and of the Very Holy Trinity for mankind.

These three stages experienced by each sufferer according to the state of individual rhythm and grace bring an astonishing interior release to that person. Is this not the paradoxical teaching reported by the Evangelists: 'Whosoever will lose his life for my sake shall find it'" (Mt 16:25)? (DC No 1858 p.833 ss).

Imprisoned and suffering the pangs of childbirth three days before giving her life for Christ, the martyr Felicity replied to her jailer: "Today, I am the one who suffers; tomorrow, Another within me will suffer for me because I shall suffer for Him." And so the *pati divina* of St Paul is realised: "I have been crucified with Christ; it is no longer I who live, but Christ who lives in me" (Gal 2:19). This communion with the sufferings of Christ, this conformity with him in his death (Phil 3:10) does not alter the dramatic character of suffering but allows the force of Redeeming Love to act in weakness.

Dom Jean-Gabriel Gelineau, O.S.B.
Master of Oblates,
Abbey of St Anne of Kergonan (Brittany)

I

Suffering

Why does God allow suffering?

Suffering in all its forms, whether moral or physical, is a trying experience which appears incomprehensible at our human level of understanding. Suffering intimidates us, subdues us. We are so perplexed that we do not dare offer any opinion on the very question that has always been a matter of primary concern: why are so many men, women and children the tragic victims of suffering throughout the world?

When one has personally endured sickness or suffering; when one has acquired the experience of age; when one has received the power of faith, the dark passageways of God lead us to the light and open up new prospects. Under such conditions the mind matures and is capable of attaining the beginning of wisdom that is the highest gift of the Spirit. But it always remains very difficult to speak of suffering and still harder to understand it. It is a matter that calls for serious thought, that cannot be circumvented and is a challenge to us all.

What is suffering?

Pope John Paul II provides us with an element of the answer in *Salvifici Doloris* (The Christian significance of suffering) – 11.2.84. In this Apostolic letter he writes that "suffering appears to belong to the transcendency of man: this is one of the points on which man is in a sense destined to surpass himself, and he is called to do so in a mysterious way."

Suffering is an endurance test that determines the quality of faith. It is through the violent storms of life that Jesus Christ reveals his presence to all those who love him. He is there, walking humbly with them, without any need to explain the whys and wherefores of misfortune. He simply leads his faithful followers to the 'holy city', where God "will wipe away every tear from their eyes; there shall be an end to death, and to mourning and crying and pain; for the old order has passed away!" (Rev 21:3,4).

A light in the darkness

Pain in all its forms is the harassing symptom of all physical disorders, diseases or injuries. But above all, it is the outrage of suffering without any apparent reason or the suffering of innocent persons that shocks us deeply because it goes beyond our scale of values. Our first reaction is often an attitude of revolt but we see that this leads to nothing. We shall become aware of the light that shines in the darkness of suffering only when we have clearly understood the need to let ourselves be led by the Lord.

The following quotation from St Augustine of Hippo offers a glimpse of the truth:

> "Almighty God in his infinite goodness would allow nothing evil to remain in his works if he were not so all-powerful and so good that he draws good from evil."
>
> *De cor. et gratia K27*

Illness and love

In many illnesses that afflict men and women today, the most disconcerting experience is to feel that the situation is utterly beyond our mental grasp. Such is the case, for example, with psychosomatic disorders, nervous breakdown, clinical depression, distress, anxiety... all these disturbances being related to the *taedium vitae* or "world weariness" of our contemporary society as much as to the particular sensitivity of the individual. When any person is laid low by some illness for which there is still no real and effective remedy, we are bound to admit that it is beyond our power to help. Even the most eloquent and reasoned arguments serve no purpose. But it is precisely our failure in this area that can have the effect of mobilising the power of faith by calling upon all that represents personal worth in a human being: the heart, and love to which sick persons are receptive witnesses.

Like Master, like disciple

On mature reflection, is a Christian's destiny not linked to that of the Master? This fundamental question must inevitably occur to believers, in particular those who suffer in their bodies or in their minds.

Jesus, on the Cross, addressed his Father by crying out with a loud voice that echoed the words of Psalm 21[22]: "Why have you forsaken me?" Jesus could have added the verse that follows: "I cry to you but you do not answer." He seems to have been neglected by a Father who preferred to remain silent rather than come to his aid. And yet we know what finally happened...

Jesus was the first to demonstrate that to love is to suffer. Thus the believer who follows the Lord is induced to "suffer while loving, to love while suffering", as St Thérèse of Lisieux so neatly put it. But she never said it was good to love suffering. And the only way of escape is the supplication of the Christian. A humble request is always granted by Christ on the Cross since Jesus, the Suffering Servant, draws all the world to him.

Good drawn from evil

In close connection with the quotation from St Augustine given earlier, the following passage appears in the above-mentioned Apostolic Letter from John Paul II: "Suffering reached its climax in the Passion of Christ... It was bound up with love... which creates good by drawing it even from evil by means of suffering... The supreme good of the Redemption of the world has been drawn from the Cross of Christ in which it continually finds its starting point..."

Further on, the Holy Father clearly states that we are all called to "share in the suffering by which Redemption was wrought" and that all human suffering has been bought back by this Redemption. "In the redemptive suffering of Christ", he adds, "Man discovers through faith his own sufferings enriched... with a new meaning: 'I have been crucified with Christ: the life I now live is not my life, but the life which Christ lives in me'" (Gal 2:19-20).

This communion with the sufferings of Christ in no way detracts from the dramatic reality of suffering. Even the beatific vision that Jesus himself retained on the Cross in no way relieved his distress. On the contrary, it increased it. St Thérèse of Lisieux wrote to her sister Céline: "We think we are capable of loving without suffering... and we should like to suffer generously, greatly... Céline, what an illusion! We should prefer never to fall? What does it matter, dear Jesus, if I fall down at each moment for by this means I see my weakness and I draw great benefit from it." St Paul had already written as much to the Corinthians: "When I am weak, then I am strong" (2 Cor 12:10).

The gift of love

In the bitter trial of men and women who have to face great moral or physical distress, it would sometimes appear that there is not even a glimmer of hope. In the same way as Christ, they experience what appears to be the silence of God and supreme dereliction. But their 'sacrifice' has a redemptive value if it is a gift of love. It is in this spirit that the full meaning of suffering can be understood. In his Apostolic Letter *Salvifici Doloris*, John Paul II assures us that "the Redemption remains constantly open to all love that is expressed in human suffering" (No. 24).

Suffering is the master of life; and no one can know himself/herself as long as he/she has not suffered. It teaches us what we are, what we are worth. This is the well travelled route to wisdom: "Know thyself" (Oracle of Delphi). And knowledge of self is a preliminary step to an intuitive knowledge of God.

Finding God by detachment

Through suffering, God puts us in an aptitude that enables us to come into his presence. We are thus filled with a sense of detachment from ourselves and our material problems. The truth is dawning upon us. We had been relying too much on the world, on other people. Through what we believe to be his silence, God enables us to experience what the great mystics such as St John of the Cross call "the nights", that is to say, apparent dereliction. We had been seeking to satisfy our selfish motives in a search for our own well-being but only misfortune comes to us. The happiness of the past has given place to the misery of today.

When I was afraid I said in my haste:
'I am cut off from your sight.'
But you heard the voice of my supplication
when I cried to you for help.

Psalm 30[31]:24

God opens up a pathway before all those in distress. He offers a safe refuge for his faithful followers and gives courage to those who keep faith in him. If we are with Christ in our sufferings, we shall render thanks for the wonders of his love. We shall recognise the greatness of the work of God who recalled his Son from the depths of the earth; and we shall ask him to live once again in him. Thus we shall be grateful and glorify his holy Name in the times to come.

You have burdened me with many and bitter troubles;
O turn and renew me;
and raise me up again from the depths of the earth.

Psalm 70[71]:20,21

The humility of God, the supreme example of Love

The living God can never give us anything but Love. The Cross reveals the love of a Father who is deeply wounded by the misery of his children on earth, always showing tenderness and mercy to all those who call upon him. In a phrase bordering on blasphemy, the revolutionary philosopher Nietzche made a shrewd guess at the truth when he wrote: "God also has his hell: it is the love he has for men." The joy of loving becomes suffering, humility and total self-giving. But St John expresses this renunciation with a strong tonality of hope:

> "God so loved the world that he gave his only Son, that whosoever believes in him should not perish but have everlasting life"
>
> *John 3:16*

God's most prodigious gift was the sacrifice of his only Son for the salvation of the world, a sacrifice that conveyed the wondrous promise of eternal life to all believers. It is a gift so precious that its real value will be revealed to us only when we enter into the fullness of God.

"If my calling as a man to enter into God's life is to be fulfilled," confides François Varillon, "then I must be made capable of loving as He does, that is to say without an atom of selfishness. To be love in my whole being, to be love and nothing else... without withdrawing into myself... Suffering is dying to self in order to be purified of all egoism."

The works of Fr Varillon are widely noted for their sound reasoning, rigour of thought and force of logic. He has left the lasting mark of a great theologian and continues to edify his readers today. Thus his book: *The Humility of God* contains this remarkable passage on the role of our Creator: "God," he said, "is not the craftsman of the world. He has not constructed it as a clockmaker constructs a clock. He does not manufacture a ready-made product. On the contrary, he withdraws in order to allow the beings created by him to spring forth by their own unaided efforts... If God were to intervene in order to prevent all tentative experiments, disturbances, resistances of inertia, tidal waves, epidemics, the world for him could be likened to an object that is manipulated. Relapsing into infantilism, our imagination would doubtless see in this a sign of greater love. But God does not love us as we should like him to love when we project our dreams onto him. He would spare us suffering but only at the cost of paternalism by which he would cease to be Love. God's trustworthiness is apparent in respect and suffering... The whole truth is that God respects us too much to prevent us from suffering as if by magic, and his self-respect is too great to spare himself the suffering caused by our own suffering.

And as to the question of evil which is the product of our freedom... how much more does that respect prove exacting under such conditions and how much deeper is that suffering of creative Love! Here we are at the heart of the mystery of the humility of God."

Thus transposed to a level which is beyond human experience, divine humility nevertheless serves as a supreme example to mankind. It is a constituent of the perfection towards which we must tend with all the strength of mind that we possess.

The egocentric force of suffering

If we are determined to defend ourselves and keep the will to win in this life of toil and trouble, we are bound to admit that our humility has its limits. To overstep these limits, we must be prepared to accept full dependence on the love of God. Only then will humility and unselfish love become capable of gaining control of the ego, thus attaining the state of spiritual self-annihilation that leads to perfection of the soul.

But we are all aware that life pulls us in the opposite direction, that it is full of pitfalls, and that suffering stands like an obstacle on the path of perfection. This mental obstruction develops an egocentric force that draws the mind inwards, relating the outside world to the sufferer's own misfortune.

The bewilderment of pain

Three questions are often present in the sick person's mind: *Why do I have to suffer? Why am I so frail? How am I going to get out of this?* And lastly, a big question is superimposed on the three others like an ultra-bold headline: WHY ME?

The search for perfection that God expects from me is no longer on the agenda. It doesn't even enter my mind. Humiliated, I fail to understand the need of humility in the face of hardship. Shattered in mind and body, I perceive no just cause for 'annihilation'. Feeling utterly confused, isolated in my interior solitude, I am in a state of passive defence, deploring the absurdity of the human condition.

And yet I well know that Christ came to share our humanity in all things except sin. By taking our sorrows upon himself, he relieves those who are sorely affflicted (cf. Is 53:4, Heb 2:18). But sick and sinful, I am unable to follow the footsteps of Christ on the road to Calvary. I see bodily suffering as an attack on my faith, on my personality, on my humanity. Pain is bewildering. It draws me into a strange and animal world that is frightening. I am living an internal drama that drives me into a frenzy like a crazed animal, that makes me roll up into a ball like some monstrous hedgehog.

Pain is a cry of incomprehension, a moan in nothingness. It saps my vitality and reduces me to tears. It focuses all my attention on myself, preventing me from thinking of anything but my own torments, suppressing both speech and prayer. I can only turn my eyes to the Cross, entreating wordlessly while obscurely understanding something of the anguish that Christ himself experienced.

But all things come to an end. And only afterwards, when brutal suffering has finally receded and my strength has timidly returned, a peaceful period of reflection can at last relieve my mind, like the calm after the storm.

When my heart was embittered
and I was wounded to the core,
I was stupid and ignorant,
no better than a beast before you.
Nevertheless I am continually with you;
you have held me by my right hand.

Psalm 72[73]:20-23

Acceptance and humility

Suffering is an abyss of unbearable solitude that seems to estrange us from God. In this black pit in which one encounters pain and the spectre of death, some persons show a rebellious attitude, others complain bitterly while feeling forsaken (despite the regular attendance of family and friends who also feel anxious). Others again have resigned themselves to the idea that suffering is the *sine qua non*, or indispensable condition of self-sacrifice.

In this struggle against the terrors of adversity, those who 'win through' in a moral sense will be able to do so only at the cost of sovereign humility, bearing in mind the example of Jacob's ladder in the Book of Genesis. In his dream, Jacob saw a ladder that extended between heaven and earth, and the angels of God ascending and descending on it. These are the steps of humility of St Benedict: as we climb the successive rungs of the ladder, we progress in humility and overcome all fear. "The ladder thus set up is our life in the world, which the Lord raises up to heaven if our heart is humbled" (R.B.7).

Then Jacob awoke from his dream and exclaimed: "Truly, the Lord is in this place and I knew it not!" (Gen 28:16).

The help of Divine Love

In our dark night, we are often tempted to protest like poor Job, that wise hebrew patriarch of exemplary piety who has to face sickness as well as great physical and emotional distress. Bereaved of all his children, stripped of his possessions, himself smitten with leprosy, and his wife advising him "to curse God and die" (Job 2:9), he gives way to despair and bewails his fate. He understands nothing. But his plunge into deep darkness is also a vision of light. His faith in the presence of the God of Love is the living spring of triumph over evil. He persistently believes in a free God who may sometimes seem unjust yet always upholds those who are laid low. He will finally see the truth, even in his misfortune: "I know that my Redeemer liveth..."[1]

The evil presence with the hideous face and the name of deep suffering can be driven away only by the power of faith. Thus the absurd is transmuted into hope and catastrophe into Redemption, by means of our submission to hardship and our detachment. The help of Divine Love can be counted on the very moment the sufferer turns away from himself or herself to go up to God in a surge of confidence.

The incomparable prospect

The acceptance of any state of affliction, of any painful experience or prospect, is greatly facilitated if I am even vaguely aware that my ordeal has a real

---

1. One of the finest recitatives of Handel's oratorio 'The Messiah' was drawn from this phrase.

and deep meaning. Should this be the case, then everything can change in the way I face up to it. Throughout any painful crisis, there is often a consciousness of the hereafter, a foreknowledge that keeps the incomparable prospect of eternal life in front of my eyes. That is where my great strength lies in the darkest moments. It is by longing for the Kingdom of God with all the ardour of my soul that I feel able to find the better side of my nature and to resign myself to the apparent absurdity of suffering.

Even tortured in the flesh and in the spirit, I have learned that sickness and suffering are conducive to discernment and that the Lord "saves the crushed in spirit" (Ps 33[34]:18). But he calls for unceasing prayer and whole-hearted resignation as instruments of his grace.

Christ has taught us that "in very truth, anyone who gives heed to my word and puts his trust in him who sent me, has eternal life" (Jn 5:24).

The gifts of God

Jesus Christ's immediate concern in our life on earth is to allow us to share in the life of the Father. He has made this clear in one of the Gospel's great sayings, assuring all his followers "that they may have life, and have it abundantly" (Jn 10:10). He goes even further by stating with insistence: "I am life" (Jn 14:6).

But so many years of our lives go by with their trail of trials and tribulations before we become conscious of the full significance of Christ's teaching.

When our minds finally grasp the truth, we become capable of perceiving to what extent Jesus is unquestionably the great healer and the gateway of life that leads to eternity.

Until that time, we had failed to understand that nothing comes from us, that life itself is given to us. We had believed like everyone else that, in order to live life to the full and overcome our difficulties, we had to rely above all on our ideas, our intentions, our courage, our willpower. Such a reasoning, however, is both misleading and fallacious.

Christ has to keep on reminding us: "If anyone wishes to be a follower of mine, he must leave self behind; he must take up his cross and come with me. Whoever cares for his own safety is lost; but if a man will let himself be lost for my sake, he will find his true self" (Mt 16:24,25).

To live life to the full means commitment to God through Jesus Christ as well as confident surrender, understanding and obedience to the spirit of faith that gives access to grace. Let us listen to Christ with both ears as he replies to the Samaritan woman: "If only you knew what God gives, and who it is that is asking you for a drink, *you* would have asked *him* and he would have given you living water" (Jn 4:10).

God is the source of all spiritual gifts, and living water is the symbol of the "inner spring that wells up to eternal life" (Jn 4:14). Through Christ, the old well of Jacob has become the Fountain of Life, that is to say the life-giving power of God in action, our source of strength and consolation.

As St Paul reminded Timothy: "God called us to a dedicated life, not for any merit of ours but of his own purpose and his own grace, which was granted to us in Christ Jesus from all eternity" (2 Tim 1:9).

Christ brings the divine truth to its fulfilment. In the account of the Transfiguration, the voice of God emphasises the glory of his Son by exhorting his disciples to listen to his teaching. The same voice now speaks to all the people of God: "This is my Son, my Beloved, on whom my favour rests; listen to him" (Mt 17:5).

God's gifts are without number, for he is the source of life, and all is grace. Our thankfulness must come before all entreaty. Our own intentions, our courageous attitudes and our efforts of will are praiseworthy only insofar as we consider them to be the consequences of the gifts we have received from God.

The new man

Prostrated and crushed by illness or suffering, by surgical operations, by long and restrictive treatments, I must not allow myself to be overwhelmed by feelings of anxiety, sadness or thoughts of death. As long as my hour has not yet come, I must say "yes" to life. Passive submission and often apprehension at the outset should give way to acceptance and finally to a state bordering on light-heartedness. I feel morally bound to revive and restore my life to the best that God has given me. The will to pull through makes it possible to abandon the 'old man' in me, to give birth to the 'new man', the man purified by the fire of suffering and endowed with new life by the spirit of God.

This 're-birth' within me enables me to feel something different from the bitter taste of death and to enter into the true life. If I have put my trust in Jesus and remained faithful through my torments, I must allow myself to be gently overcome by his spirit of peace, of love and of courage.

The divine power which is spirit conditions the Christian life and recalls the reply given by Christ to Nicodemus: "It is spirit that gives birth to spirit. Do not be astonished, then, when I tell you that you must be born again" (Jn 3:6,7).

Fighting the good fight

The greatness of man passes through his participation in the work of God and through his fight against evil and injustice. The whole of humanity is called upon to support a common struggle against evil, violence and hatred on the basic principles of liberty, fraternity, equality and justice which can alone lead to peace.

This new world war conducted on all fronts for a closer understanding between peoples of all nations is the same as the inner battle that each one of us has to fight on a smaller scale in order to defeat the forces of evil within ourselves. Thus the 'good fight' within us restores the value of an impaired life and body by endowing them with unity, freedom and a meaning that conforms to the teachings of Christ.

The price of human life

Christ is in the main thread of events that concern us, in our relationship with others, as well as in our misfortunes. He makes use of our daily lives, of our ups and downs, to bring us to seek the truth beyond the deceptive appearances of darkness, and to show us clearly that we are without price in the eyes of God. Each and every human being has the right to affirm the undisputed truth: "God loves me personally and with wonderful kindness as if I were the only one in the world to inherit eternal life. But, being in God's image, I cannot look at others without thinking that they are of priceless value in *my* eyes!"

The source of a radiant faith

The Son of God came into the world, not to destroy all distress but to bring relief by sharing it with us. The presence of the living Saviour was, and remains, the final and definite answer to all our misgivings: "I am the Way, the Truth and the Life" (Jn 14:6). The way out of worry, the victory of love, is through the risen Lord. We are thoroughly renewed and strengthened in mind and body, not by the sufferings of Christ in themselves, but by the hope made manifest in the very depth of his sufferings. It is through the hope that springs from Christ that our faith can shine forth with a new radiance.

Healing of mind and body

When faith is strong and ardent, the Lord always comes to our aid. Faith induces healing of ailments just as a magnetic pole attracts an unlike pole. One is necessary for the other, just as attentive silence is necessary in order to listen to the spoken word. When the abyss of deep distress and dereliction opens wide, then the torrent of divine love rushes in.

"Jesus, Master, take pity on us." The healing of the ten men with leprosy was the answer to their faith. Only one of them (a foreigner) turned back, "praising God with a loud voice. He fell down on his face at the Lord's feet, giving him thanks" (Lk 17:13-15).

Many people recover from physical disorders. But if only one person glorifies God, that person will be saved. The entire being will be restored to both integrity and dignity.

"It is indeed my will; be healed and purified" (Lk 5:13). How we should all like to hear these words!

The finest fruit of faith

In difficult and distressing circumstances, God asks his children to turn to him since their well-being is his sole concern. Whole-hearted trust, acknowledgement of his unfailing love and the willing obedience that goes with it, offer a spiritual response of the soul to God's call. It is the offering of oblation in a heart-to-heart relationship with the Creator: "You must love the Lord your God with all your heart, and with all your soul, and with all your strength" (Deut 6:5).

"Father, into your hands I commit my spirit" (Lk 23:46); (Ps 30[31]:5). Though uttered by Jesus in his dying breath on the Cross, this is not a cry of despair but of total submission to the will of the Father. It is a supreme example, expressed in the prayer that Christ himself has taught us: "Thy will be done".

Our best response to the will of God is precisely to show him that we are ready to commit ourselves into his hands at all times and without hanging back. In this way we anticipate the Resurrection of Jesus Christ, whose invincible power enables us to put up a determined fight against the enemy within us and at last to find a new zest for life.

Although it had hitherto appeared to us that we had been put to rout by the superior forces of adversity, the *anima divina* within us at last begins to gain the upper hand. The grace of healing in mind and body is the finest fruit of faith: "My daughter, your faith has cured you. Go in peace, free for ever from this trouble" (Mk 5:34).

Expiation that has become redemption

The experience of physical suffering, in the same way as the experience of love, enables every disciple of Christ to gain a better understanding of the meaning of life that is dependent on the life of the Master. We begin to grasp the relationship that exists between suffering humanity and the agony of the Passion.

Christ on the Cross had to face the same agonising questions and the same inner conflicts as anyone who is touched by personal tragedy. Since he came to share our human condition, and "since he himself has passed through the test of suffering, he is able to help those who are meeting their test now" (Heb 2:18).

It is here that the ground fog lifts before our eyes, giving us a fleeting vision of the future that God holds in store for those who are lost (cf. Mk 8:35; Lk 19:10).

In accordance with God's plan that is revealed to us in the Gospels, his Son was not sent into the world to explain the enigma of unjust suffering "but that through him the world might be saved" (Jn 3:17). By accepting the ultimate trial of the Crucifixion, by attaining the heart of suffering that is injustice, Jesus has abolished the secular concept of expiation of sin by suffering, transforming it into the doctrine of universal redemption.

A unique occasion

Thus suffering is neither a sanction, nor a discipline, nor a means of atonement for any misdeed. It is a unique occasion to resemble Christ more closely, for he is the 'Man of Sorrows'. I no longer ask myself *"Why me?"* I am never alone. If I am suffering and worried, I know that Christ is suffering with me. He has become pain and suffering for me and within me. Pain, doubt, anxiety, solitude, self-pity: they are all present in Christ, and Christ is totally present within me when I suffer.

The general meaning of Christ's teaching is crystal-clear: he carries the Cross for all those who come to him in distress. If I am incapable of visualising Christ in this act of divine mercy, then I am equally unable to see him re-living in my troubled being and I have spent a lifetime looking elsewhere for the Spirit of Love that has always been present in the depths of my own soul!

A lighter burden

If we are true followers of Christ, we cannot do otherwise than to share in his sufferings. When there is no escape from the ordeal of pain, we have to crawl into it with courage, enduring it with the spirit of our suffering Saviour. Then he reproduces himself in us, so much so that our sufferings become his and we reproduce ourselves in him.

By offering a subdued spirit in an ailing body, we share in the work of redemption by Jesus Christ who suffered and died for us. Even now, when we are weighed down by misfortune, he bears our sorrows and endures our torments, thus relieving our heavy burden of misery.

We can still hear his warm and comforting words: "Come to me, all who labour and are heavy laden, and I will give you rest. Take my yoke upon you, and learn from me; for I am gentle and lowly in heart, and you will find rest for your souls. For my yoke is easy, and my burden is light" (Mt 11:28-30).

Compassion and salvation

Through Jesus Christ, the Passion has become compassion, pointing the way to salvation by a mystical communion, a communication and a dialogue between God and man. Thus, even while in the throes of death on the Cross, Christ promised eternal life to the penitent thief who was crucified beside him. Though put to the same torture, he had simply asked to be remembered by "the man who had done nothing wrong".

In the cruel grip of pain and anguish, the suffering servants of today who draw comfort and hope from the source of love can only bear a greater resemblance to their beloved Master. Unwavering trust in the Lord under the most trying conditions sanctifies the soul and gives a foretaste of the sweetness of Heaven.

"Lord Jesus, we were close to death. By your death, you bring us back to life."

—.—.—

Facing an insidious illness: clinical depression

A final cause for concern is the problem of psychic suffering. Often experienced as an internal breakdown that shakes its victims to the core, its complex and incapacitating nature has become the subject of much discussion and controversy. But do we have the right to comment when we only know that the number of different forms of depression is almost equal to the number of victims?

On condition that we remain humble in the face of this mystery, there is nothing to prevent us from contributing our own modest opinion. Our sole aim here is to throw a little more light on an obscure and intricate problem and to try to bring a ray of hope in an illness that is still too often misunderstood and underestimated.

Clinical depression is in fact a nervous and psychic illness. Devaluation of self, a feeling of failure, loss of taste for life, the symptoms are legion. Moral suffering reduces otherwise healthy persons to a state of exhaustion, of prostration and despair. Sufferers are rarely able to treat the condition without professional help. But what they do require above all is a strong dose of love and tenderness in order to recover. A kind of apathy has invaded the whole personality, concealing indefinable anguish that is lived with in silence, that makes these afflicted persons incapable of facing up to things, plunging them into a state of black despondency. People who suffer from depression may even lose their bearings in religion and lose their faith in God.

Medical assistance may be sought but there remains a metaphysical anguish that seems to be feared even by specialists. All too frequently, psychotherapy fails to drive out this insidious evil that dwells in the mind. For who is able to probe the depths of the soul? Who can understand the resonance of anguish or suspect the amplitude of an internal upheaval?

Assuming that the depressive person is a man, he has been afflicted in the intimacy of his being and he tells himself it is *his* suffering. His family circle can do nothing about it. He sinks into an obstinate silence. He is prey to an inner conflict: on the one hand he feels attracted towards those who support him and love him. On the other hand he feels the need for withdrawal into himself, into the inner refuge of his mind.

Life is a series of trials and periods of respite. In adversity, many women show a tendency to confide their worries to others while men often limit their replies to a laconic "I'm fine" whereas in actual fact it may be quite the contrary. The members of their families know it all to well. Living with a 'depressive' can be a perplexing experience of apparent contradictions that only serve to aggravate the general feeling of helplessness.

A state of depression conceals suffering that often goes back to early childhood and makes the patient incapable of coming to terms with himself. Aware of the fact that he is not in a normal state, racked with doubts and anguish for no valid reason, he appears to feel utterly neglected and forlorn despite all the concern that may be shown for his welfare.

The sad, doleful expression of a person who is suffering in this way is the outward sign of an internal fight against gloomy thoughts that range from the greyness of sadness to the blackness of despair.

What is there to be done? The main thing is to try to trace the cause of the problem, to localise the conflict, then to externalise the depression before it becomes unbearable.

The gloomy thoughts that invade the mind and may be termed forces of evil end up by dominating the personality as long as they meet with no resistance. They can be made to lose their hold only by confronting them, that is to say by exposing the darkness of distress to the broad light of day as one would open one's heart to the Lord. It is only by becoming aware of the ill contained in illness of this type that the heart will finally be freed from its prison.

Those who were bowed down by distress will then be able to stand up straight again. Thankful for the love they receive, they will no longer belittle themselves in defeat or enclose themselves in a sombre bastion of defensive solitude.

Snatched from the clutches of Satan, the freed believer will be restored to serenity and peace of mind, having been filled with new understanding by the light of Christ who said: "I am the light of the world. No follower of mine shall wander in the dark. He shall have the light of life" (Jn 8:12).

It is this light that will penetrate the secret of all anxiety and help to discover the truth about oneself. Jesus Christ also said: "The truth will make you free" (Jn 8:32). The freedom to which he refers here is that of the filial relationship between the believer and God through Christ who delivers sinners from the bondage of falsehood. But this relationship must be lived in faith and with the absolute certainty that his inexhaustible love ensures victory over evil.

St Peter speaks with compassion to those who are frail and feeble in their distress: "Humble yourselves then under God's mighty hand and he will lift you up in due time. Cast all your anxieties on him, for he cares about you" (cf. 1 Pet 5:6-7).

Why are you cast down, O my soul,
And why are you disquieted within me?

Hope in God: for I shall again praise him,
my help and my God.

Psalm 41[42]:6

Grounded on Holy Scripture, our faith reminds us insistently that he who loves is beloved of God. Whoever continues to love through all the trials that have to be endured, that person's life can never be a failure, and all the less so since clinical depression is often a Way of the Cross. St Paul helps us in our faltering footsteps on this Way by assuring us that nothing, not even tribulation or distress, "can separate us from the love of God that is in Christ Jesus our Lord" (Rom 8:35,39).

May all those who remain unshakeable in their faith 'come wind, come weather' be capable of sharing this assurance and of holding the true course of hope, even in the murkiest gloom of existence.

II

The silence of Infinite Love

The universal quest

God keeps silence in order to be able to speak. When the listener becomes aware of the eloquence of silence, the voice of the Lord our God can then be heard.

The Word of God is expressed infallibly and without cease through the deep need that men and women have always felt since the dawn of civilisation. They are driven by an irresistible urge to assuage their thirst for the Absolute, by an ardent desire to know the purpose that accounts for their existence and to catch a glimpse of their destiny. They pester themselves with continual questionings about the meaning of life and death, about the enigma of life hereafter, about the history of the world and of themselves as human beings. What guiding force can raise such questions in their minds if it is not the founder of the world? This universal quest could clearly have been lodged in the inmost depths of consciousness only by the Creator of the human race.

The Revelation of Love

The quest for a Supreme Being who is both personal and all-powerful imparts unity to the history of humanity in the purpose of God.

Jahweh, the God of the Old Testament, revealed himself as a God who sends out his word and grants the gift of speech while remaining hidden and respecting the freedom of men and women.

Since the beginnings of their history, the tribes of Israel understood that, if they committed themselves completely to his service while accepting all the solitude, suffering and even death that might ensue, Yahweh would emerge from his silence and come forward to meet his chosen people. The starting point of the encounter was the silent space of the Holy of Holies that was filled with the glory of God.

Our belief is that God manifests his presence in the space of Christian faith. In that space, the plenitude of essential silence nourishes the word. Those who lend an attentive ear, those who make themselves available in the presence of a Father whose name is Love, enter into a state of sweet and peaceful union with him. But he allows himself to be heard only in the grace of silence that dwells in the inmost recesses of the soul.

The commitment of a deep relationship

"Heaven does not speak." This was one of the teachings of the great Chinese philosopher Kung Futzu, better known as Confucius. Far from being without religious ideals, he respected the All-powerful Love of Heaven (*T'ien*) that has no need to speak in order to be understood.

As Christians, we can find discernment only in the apparent silence of our Father. God does not reveal himself in majesty and triumph but in the weakness of the Crucifixion, where he brings salvation and eternal life to humankind, thus by making manifest his unconditional love for us all.

Finally, he reveals himself in silence as a God who is both transcendent and immanent, close and familiar, a God who has committed himself once and for all to a deep and personal relationship with us.

A Father who never leaves us

The humility of God can be judged by his silence, in which he conveys to us his loving respect, his greatness, and his proximity. The truth of this was perceived by the prophet Elijah on Mount Horeb, the 'Mountain of God': the Lord was not in the wind, nor in the earthquake, nor in the fire. After the fire, however, there was "the sound of deep silence" (1 Kings 19:12) (Hebrew text). And it was with a still, small voice that the Lord spoke to him in order to deliver him from his distress.

In the last part of the work cited in the previous chapter, Fr Varillon recalls the different stages of the life of Christ, in which the silence of God is a constant and significant characteristic. He observes that "Jesus who heals the sick is the same Jesus who, at the threshold of his ministry, refused to change stones to bread, and who, tomorrow on the Cross, will be aware of the Father's presence only in the mode of silence and of his absence. Between the inaugural scene and the last act, the entire life of Jesus is stamped with the seal of non-intervention of God. In this way his death never ceases to be prophesied. Paradoxically, it is in this cryptic form that his thaumaturgic activity[1] is expressed. Its style is the same as his word, the point of which pierces the silence to signify the kenotic[2] depth of God. His word is born of silence – thirty obscure years and entire nights of solitude and prayer during his public life – and reverts to silence when at Calvary the Father and the Son fail to engage in a dialogue. But their silence is neither remoteness nor opacity. It is precisely the word that qualifies it as the essence of the reality of God in his proximity. It affirms that this silence is not nothingness, but fullness."

His silence is a presence

If God sometimes gives us the impression of remaining mute and impassive even when we call to him, it is because our rationalistic way of thinking too often prevents us from perceiving the deep

---

1. The performance of miracles.
2. In its first sense, *kenosis* is the self-abasement of Christ or the partial annihilation of his divine nature in his incarnation (cf. Phil 2,7). In the second sense considered here, the *kenosis of God* is the deep humility of the Father who consents to the sacrifice of the Son for the salvation of the world.

meaning of eternal truth. In order to allow us to know him, he does not speak to us as we would speak to each other. "I am that I am" is the name by which he describes himself. He is absolute light. He lights up our lives and gives us understanding. He puts us in readiness for prayer, in a frame of mind such that we become sure of his love and strong in our faith. His silence is a presence of which he is the heart.

From the source of all goodness flow peace of the soul and consent to what we know and recognise as the divine will. This deep silence of the Beloved is the essential background for a deep spiritual communion that enables us to discover his presence, to turn our thoughts to him and to avoid needless talk. As we know only too well, the spoken word is a trap and it is easy to say one thing while thinking another. The abundance of the heart is revealed by words. But the abundance of words conceals the bottom of the heart. It is not by talking at length with a wealth of words and phrases that we shall be heard more readily. We must learn to keep a watch on our tongue. If we refer to the Rule of St Benedict, we find the same precept followed by the conclusion: "The disciple's part is to be silent and to listen" (R.B.6).

The vital force of faith

The example and teaching of the Master make it clear to any faithful and assiduous disciple that faith is expressed most of the time in a silence that is not an absence of either sound or speech but is an opening and an expectation of the life-giving breath of the Spirit.

One must not expect to go into a trance or into any state of concentration that might interfere with the normal course of everyday life. On the contrary, true attentive faith is a vital force that frees one's personality and produces an outward radiance.

The believer discovers that God is present in a silence that is an invitation to do likewise, that the Divine Presence is in all places and that "the eyes of the Lord are everywhere" (Prov 15:3). The Word of God is a gap pierced in an apparent silence and this silence is a communion with his love.

The example of the Son

The Father also wants to teach us that it is through the intrinsic value of silence that the Word can be treasured in our hearts. He demonstrated this truth in the life of the Son who spent thirty years at Nazareth, as noted earlier, but was to devote only his last three years to his public ministry. The ratio can readily be expressed: ten periods of silence to one period of preaching. In the course of only three years, the shortest but the greatest period of his outstanding life and mission, our Lord opened the gates of new life to the world.

"In him was life, and the life was the light of men. The light shines in the darkness, and the darkness has not overcome it" (Jn 1:4,5).

In the vast chaos of the primeval universe, the Word of Life already shone in the darkness from the beginning which was so strikingly described by St John. He was "the image of the invisible God" (Col 1:15), "the effulgence of God's splendour" (Heb 1:3).

Appearing from the soundless depths of night, he comes to flood the twisting path of Man with his true light. Everything behind him remains shrouded in deep shadow. As soon as his word is spoken, everything in the world, everything that is within us, is organised and given a meaning. He alone is our guide. Called by him, we know who we are. But he whom we call Lord, who is *he*?

"Who do men say that I am?" he asked his disciples. Their varying replies give us an idea of the mystery that surrounded his person. "And you, who do *you* say that I am?" (Mk 8:29). Alone amongst all the disciples, Peter answered him promptly: "You are the Messiah." But as soon as he heard this reply, Jesus gave strict orders not to repeat it to anyone. It was his 'secret'. His earthly mission had not yet been fully revealed. His hour had not yet come. The true name of the man who had come to liberate Israel as people then believed had to lapse into silence.

The truth could only advance in muffled and discreet steps. Jesus Christ alone knew the truth of Peter's reply. But even the name of the Messiah could not encompass the immense mystery of the Creation, in which the Heavenly Father envelops the "Word made Flesh" in a silence that reveals the divine wisdom.

He who was the "light of men", the light that shone in the darkness, came into a world of sound and fury. His cry in the night lasted the space of a humble and sublime birth that was to bring a promise to the world. But the promise is buried away and the Infant King becomes the anonymous child of Nazareth. Jesus keeps quiet, allowing his humble and laborious existence to speak for itself, announcing to the world that he shares the condition of all men and women without exception. His humility is stronger than the hubbub of speech and is expressed without words.

Jesus Christ emerged from a background of silence to proclaim the spiritual reign of God in our lives: "For I have come down from heaven, not to do my will, but the will of him who sent me" (Jn 6:38).

Listening to the Father

Our efforts must therefore be directed to a constant search for the will of God who loves us, and who appears to be silent only insofar as we ourselves seem incapable of remaining silent as we should do, precisely in order to stay 'tuned-in', to listen carefully and to do his will.

If only we were capable of turning our minds to God in contemplation, of receiving him in our hearts and keeping quiet, if we were vigilant and attentive, we should pierce the veil. God would reveal himself to us continually. We would understand his action and all that happens to us, even events that may previously have seemed unjust in our dim-sighted eyes. To all that confronts us, we would then say *"Dominus est"* – It is the Lord!

Under all circumstances of our worldly life, we would find that we are receiving a gift from God, though well aware that we are no more than very weak instruments whose power can lie solely in faith, hope and love.

According to Fr Jean-Pierre Caussade, "If we had faith, we should be kindly and gratefully disposed towards all creatures, we should caress them, we should be thankful to them in our hearts for what they serve and make so favourable to our perfection, applied by the hand of God."

God's pact

God has concluded a pact with men and women and has therefore entered into a harmonious relationship of reconciliation through Jesus Christ. This pact of sovereign grace promises salvation and eternal life but also makes an irrevocable pledge of fidelity to the people of God.[1]

In his New Covenant in which Jesus Christ is the Mediator, we discover throughout our lifetime the bountiful goodness of Providence in which God fills us with his grace, guarding and keeping us with constant and tireless concern for our well-being. For our Creator is constant, unchanging, eternal. He cannot be compared with the human beings that we are. "Our thoughts are not his thoughts, neither are our ways his ways" (cf. Is 55:8).

1. Isaiah 55:3, Luke 1,67-79, John 3:15, John 10:28, Acts 28:28, Romans 6:23, 2 Thessalonians 2:13, Hebrews 9:15, 1 John 2:25.

Misunderstanding of the terms

Too often, we commit the error of anthropomorphism by attempting to attribute to God the same thoughts as our own. It is not for us to transpose to God a personal experience that is too often tainted with vanity. God cannot be reduced to our small scale. Our knowledge of ourselves can never be more than partial. And yet the temptation may prove to be too strong. We are not always prepared to admit that by taking a caricature of God for God himself, we do not see him as he is, and we refuse to accept the interference of a liberty other than our own. The terms of God's pact are not complied with.

On his side of the agreement, God does not give way to our whims and fancies, or even to our legitimate aspirations if we fail to show that we are capable of fulfilling his divine laws before he grants our requests in his turn.

Compliance with the terms

If we grasp the eternal significance of the words of Christ in the night of Gethsemane by repeating to ourselves "Not my will, but Thine be done", the Truth will at once dawn upon our minds. The Father has only one will, that of making all things contribute to the good of those who love him. In his absolute paternity, he undertakes to keep his covenant with all human beings while remaining free from the traps of human language. He only asks for our consent. He chose us before the birth of the world to respond with joy and humility to his eternal call and to his loving will.

The response that God hopes for and seeks from us above all is that we shall follow the footsteps of Christ, leading a life of love in the way that he has taught us. Life is an open door to those who understand that all God's promises find their fulfilment in the person of his Son.

In the name of the knowledge of Love, God suffered self-sacrifice[1] for our salvation, in the unspoken terms of one who loves without counting the cost: "You are the one that counts and not I." If we show ourselves capable of saying – and meaning – the same from our own standpoint while being fully prepared to prove our trust, we shall have complied with the terms of his pact and shall be able to enter into a new life with God.

Our greatest joy will then be to come closer to him and to transform our hearts, thus discovering that the silence of God is the silence of Infinite Love. This is the ever-flowing spring of the Gift of God that wells up to eternal life, and to which Christ is constantly calling each one of his faithful followers.

As I prepare to come joyfully in answer to his call, I nevertheless feel a deep need to express my perplexed state of mind, fully conscious of my unworthiness.

---

1. Cf. Phil 2:8. See previous note on the *"kenosis of God"* (p.46).

"But Lord, how can I drink from such a deep and generous fountain of grace? How can I restrain my impatience which resists the call of your Word when it spreads again in silence in my mind? If your purpose is to be fulfilled in me, you must impregnate my unruly nature with the gentleness of your soothing silence. Make this divine silence go down into the depths of my soul, that it may then move upwards in homage to you. I shall then at last be capable of overcoming my deafness and of straining my ears to the limit until your silence is transmuted to a murmur of love. And then I shall be able to say like St Thérèse of Lisieux in her last moments: 'I don't repent of having abandoned myself to Love. Oh! No, I don't repent of it, on the contrary!'"

Greatness and mercy

Our Father never gives up communicating with his children but he does so only in the soundless speech of self-effacement. His Omnipotence is not what one might imagine. It is an infinity of effacement in an infinite power of love. The power and the glory of love are revealed only when the beloved child discerns the greatness of a Father who is already intimately present within that child. Thus our understanding of his exquisite word emerges from the silent encounter of love in our hearts.

If the believer allows this divine word to penetrate his mind and permits its fulfilment in his life, he will find in it both dynamism and conversion by Christ: "If a man loves me, he will keep my word, and my Father will love him, and we will come to him and make our home with him" (Jn 14:23).

By acknowledging and receiving this word, we shall know how much the Father loves and welcomes his children in the greatness of his grace and the nearness of his mercy. For this reason we shall be able to state with assurance that we exalt his holy Name, that we love him with all our heart and with all our mind when we turn to him and give him our reply of commitment and faith.

Let us simply bear in mind that it is God's call that makes it possible for us to reply and that he is not a prisoner of our words, of our desires, of our definitions and our dogmas. He surpasses by far all that may be said of him since his wonders are radically different from ours.

> "The greatness of the work of God far exceeds the power of the human language... Let us therefore rejoice in our inadequacy to speak of such great mercy..."
>
> *St Leo, Sermon 9, 'Nativity'*

God speaks to us in our heart

In the silence of our Creator, there is a rich store of beauty that is a source of unending joy. In the depths of our soul, God speaks to us unceasingly and in a thousand ways. But we often have the middle name of Obstinate and therefore fail to recognise the signs he sends us, though they are there for all to see. The Book of Wisdom seems to confirm and strengthen this assertion: "Vanity lies in the nature of men. They live in ignorance of God and, in the good things before their eyes, they have not been capable of discerning him who really is. They have failed to recognise the Artificer though they have observed his works. For the greatness and beauty of created things gives us a corresponding idea of their Creator" (Wis 13:1-5).

God is a beggar for love

Let God be loved for what he is, the supreme God made man, remote yet close by, Almighty but accessible and tolerant, hidden while revealing himself, and achieving his purpose with the infinite patience of his grace that acts within us. By humility and discretion which are inseparable from his love, he wants to show us that he is also a beggar for our love, for the free act of faith that we express in prayer. If it should so happen that God does not answer us, our plea is never refused or dismissed. He is reticent only in order to encourage us to persevere. For we have to understand that our faith can grow only through the patient and confident attitude in which we put ourselves in his hands.

We may be quite certain that God loves us just as we are. He is fully aware of all our imperfections, our weaknesses, and all those misdeeds that we always say we shall never commit again. We shall probably never be saints, nor shall we be angels. It therefore serves no purpose to wait until we are perfect in order to give our heart to God.

Our Eternal Father asks us to give him all our

affection. But we shall be able to love him only as we are, without make-believe, in the poverty of our heart as in our faithfulness. He takes no notice of our talents, our knowledge, our intellectual aptitude. To him even our virtues are of small account since he knows that, by giving them to us, we are so weak that they turn too often into self-esteem.

What our Father would like above all is to see love rising from the depths of our misery and filling the present moment with the little that we have to give him. Like a beggar, the Master of the Universe knocks discreetly at the door of our heart. The only real injury inflicted on Love would be to hesitate to open our hearts, to doubt, to lack confidence. This door can be opened only from the interior.

Let us therefore think of our Heavenly Father who is waiting patiently, outside in the silence of the night. Let us allow him to come into our hearts. And then, when we are suffering, he will give us strength and courage. When we show him that we rely on him for everything, we may expect to receive an abundance of grace beyond our wildest dreams.

The ways of the Lord: Job's reply

In the outstanding life story of Job which has already been referred to in chapter I, the silence of God is the ultimate bane of an existence pursued by misfortune. But faith finally re-asserts itself and Job's growing assurance implies his submission to the divine wisdom of the Almighty. To Job is then granted the privilege of hearing a hymn to the Creation in which all the prodigious wonders of Nature are reviewed.

In an enlightened reply, Job has to admit his own insignificant smallness before the sovereign greatness of the Lord and then makes his final confession: "I have uttered what I did not understand, things too wonderful for me which I did not know... I had heard of thee by the hearing of the ear, but now my eye sees thee" (Job 42:3-5).

Having greatly suffered yet learned to speak humbly and rightly, Job is restored to peace and contentment by a just God who satisfies him with long life.

Our reply today

In the reassuring stillness and beauty of Nature, we can hear God *super voces aquarum multarum*: "Above the clamour of the many waters, of the superb breakers of the sea, the Lord on high is mighty" (Ps 92[93]:5). We can see God in the vastness of space and the psalmist gives us a most admirable vision of the glory and the majesty of God that are revealed in the heavens:

> The heavens declare the glory of God
> and the firmament proclaims his handiwork;
> One day tells it to another
> and night to night communicates knowledge.
>
> There is no speech or language
> nor are their voices heard;

Yet their sound has gone out through all the
world
and their words to the ends of the earth.

Psalm 18[19]:1-4

God speaks to us in our souls by the love of his Almighty power and by the world about us. No better ourselves than pale shadows of Job, our reply today can only be still more modest:

"You challenge us through the greatness of your works, the events that gladden us and those that sadden us. We know that you never stop talking to us in our hearts as you once spoke to your Son who was willingly heard only by simple people without pretension and without pride. Father, you who are never anything but Love, open our eyes that we may see you, unstop our ears that we may hear you! Teach us to read the signs you send us! Grant that we may learn to perceive your holy Presence through life and through death, through suffering and healing, through sadness and joy, through the work and the aspirations of men and women today."

Interference that masks the Word

Just as a transmitting station can be received by a transistor radio only if this receiver is correctly tuned to the transmitter frequency, so God can be clearly heard only if we are correctly tuned to him. One has to be on the same 'wavelength'. He has to be sought in order to be found. God is in fact present, but the interference is such that his signal is often inaudible. In a deafening cacophony of noises, shrill music and ceaseless chatter, the peaceful voice of God can no longer be heard.

There are many people who dismiss the concept of an Essential Being by comparing him with the vacuum that Nature abhors. He is a synonym of nothingness in their minds and silence to them is disturbing. The attractions of the modern world are incompatible with prayer and with contemplation which is free reception of divine grace in the sanctuary of the soul.

The basic principle of faith

How can a message be received when it is transmitted to us only in a 'tenuous silence'? The primary requirement is to achieve silence of the heart, for only that kind of silence is capable of hearing the silence of the Spirit. This divine and tranquil murmur can only be perceived when the soul is in peace, unified and free from all unwanted noise.

Peace of the soul can be attained only by passive contemplation. The soul knows God only insofar as it is a 'capacity for God'. It therefore feels a deep need to receive him in order to grow. But it is only by destitution and extreme poverty that the soul will become receptive, ready to receive everything from God alone. "God alone suffices" since the *rest* is nothingness. The soul will progress beyond words and beyond the world to the silence of a relationship of love in which it will fuse in God.

In this true silence in which God gives himself,

the Word becomes clear: "My Father and I are one" (Jn 10:30). In our hidden but hopeful hearts we give thanks and praise the Lord: *tibi silentium laus*, for you silence is praise.

Through this new consciousness of the divine Presence, we receive the Gospel message in an attitude of very simple availability, in submission to God with the love that he arouses within us, and in a constant endeavour to make our life conform to that of Christ, which is the basic principle of faith.

"I always do what is pleasing to him" (Jn 8:29), said the Son of God, dearly beloved in the highest sense. To listen lovingly to God is the 'be all and end all' of the believer. The silence of the individual ego enables God's human creatures to hear the soft divine voice that speaks unceasingly in their hearts, revealing himself to them through the Son. For as St John of the Cross has told us: "The Father has said only one word, and that word was his Son. He has always said it in an endless silence. And it is in this silence that it can be heard by the soul" (Spiritual sentences and maxims, 217).

Pax Christi

The mystery of silence that is the Divine Word can be fathomed only by reaching down into the interior space of faith. This space is favourable to prayer since "the kingdom of God is within you" (Lk 17:21).

The disciple who remains a devoted listener must rule out any discordant preoccupation, any upsetting of harmony, any prejudice, any pride. The storm of passion must be calmed and any interference of extraneous noise must be reduced to zero. That is the price of peace.

By a growing acceptance of the divine will, the soul will allow itself to be pervaded by the peace of Christ and will enter into communion with him, exclaiming with St Thomas: "My Lord and my God!"

During the Last Supper, Jesus Christ said: "Peace I leave with you; my peace I give to you; not as the world gives do I give to you. Let not your hearts be troubled, neither let them be afraid" (Jn 14:27). The peace of the Lord is not a superficial gesture but the expression of deep sincerity and serenity which attains the confines of the human heart, that complex reality which symbolises all that is most living and loving in man, woman or child.

The peace of Christ gives an intuitive perception of the image of God in the divine face of Christ or of any fellow being, the face that can emerge even from the tragic circumstances of suffering. It is a peace that urges us "to seek only the glory of God in all things" (1 Pet 4:11); (R.B.57).

The reign of silence

In this enlightened depth of silence that is the accompaniment of life, in the pure consent and intimate adherence to the Wisdom of the Father, we will discover the secret of the creative word that brings us into being. We will at last be able to find peace inhabited by the Presence, which is a communion of two silences. We will finally understand that it was not the silence of God that weighed heavily on our minds. It was the difficulty we experienced in withdrawing into our own silence in order to receive and interiorise the Word. For this Word demands of all people that they should turn away from evil, abound in love, and forgive one another.

The serenity of silence in the quiet night of the soul builds up all our confidence, the confidence that love gives when it has become so great that it can no longer be expressed in words but in the heart.

In this blessed and everlasting night in which the silence of Infinite Love reigns supreme, the Beloved is All, absolute transcendency, fundamental Presence, supernatural knowledge, ineffable splendour beyond all joy and all wonder that can be expressed.

The eager acceptance of Love

Meeting the Father thus takes place in a silence of night, a waiting period filled with reverential fear that turns into an eager acceptance of Love, a surrender to the Absolute, and a deepening of self. In this divine silence, we are drawn towards a full transparency of light in which God wants to inspire us with courage and intelligence of the heart. It is on this royal road that the Father guides us to the refuge of the soul which is the place of prayer.

III

The path of prayer

What God expects of us

By turning to the Lord in our distress or simply in our failure to understand, we shall obtain a reply only if we call upon him 'in truth', that is to say with sincerity, fidelity, steadfastness in faith, and assiduity in prayer.

The Lord expects us to come to him at all times, in sickness and in health, "...for the Lord is good. He is a sure refuge for those who look to him in the day of trouble" (Nahum 1:7).

Such is the power of attraction of human progress in the material fields of technology, entertainment, comfort and well-being that we show a marked tendency to give them priority in our minds. But all too often, when things are going badly, when the "devices and desires of our own hearts" have failed to come up to expectations and we are weighed down with overwhelming worries, many of us resort to prayer as a last expedient, but without conviction.

Where is our faith? Let us be fearless and trusting. The only effect of anxiety is to pile sorrow upon sorrow. We must recall Christ's appeal for confidence: "Which of you, by being anxious, can add a foot to his height?" (Mt 6:27).

Psalm 90[91] is among the most consoling in the Psalter. It assures us that, no matter what the trouble or the danger may be, we have only to ask. The pathos of a God waiting – and longing – to be asked! To be trusted!

> He who dwells in the shelter of the Most High:
> who abides under the shadow of the Almighty,
> he will say to the Lord:
> 'You are my refuge and my stronghold:
> my God in whom I trust.'
>
> *Psalm 90[91]:1,2*

Without God, there can be no comfort, no effective help, no lasting remedy. Let us therefore resolve to give top priority to prayer:

> O Lord I call to you: make haste to help me;
> and hear my voice when I cry,
> Let my prayer be as incense before you;
> and the lifting up of my hands
> as the evening sacrifice.
>
> *Psalm 140[141]:1,2*

What must we ask?

St Paul himself admits: "We do not know how we ought to pray" (Rom 8:26). And indeed there are many of us who wonder: "Just how am I to call to the Lord? How do I come to him in prayer? What exactly should I ask?"

In a letter once received from a very devout lady whose husband had been suffering from a very long and serious nervous breakdown, this very simple but admirable phrase seemed to shine forth like a beacon in the encircling gloom: *"It seems to me that the best course is to ask God to lead us on HIS road, to have great faith in him. knowing that he will be with us..."*

The example of the Curé d'Ars

The Curé d'Ars could serve as a model for us all. In the course of an excessively busy life, he prayed constantly and maintained an unfailing union with God, asking him at all times to lead him on his road. He was inexhaustible when he spoke of the joys and benefits of prayer. Let us just listen a moment to what he still has to say to us today: "Man is a pauper who needs to ask everything of God... Prayer, that is the whole joy of man on earth."

He himself experienced this joy over a long period of time and has disclosed its very simple secret: "There is no need for us to talk so very much in order to pray well", he explained to his parishioners. "We know that the good Lord is there... we just open our hearts to him; we take pleasure in his holy presence. That's the best prayer of all."

In the final analysis, this all inevitably points to the prayer above all others that Jesus himself has taught us: "Your will be done", with emphasis on *your*, since, if I am to deny myself in order to follow you, Lord, it is not *my* will that counts but yours alone.

A love story

Prayer is essentially a love story. Under the inspiration of grace, we open our hearts freely and frankly, without deceit or hypocrisy. It is time for a heart-to-heart talk with Our Father, with "Him whom my soul loves", as the Bride sings in the Canticle of Canticles. We praise and bless the Lord. We give him thanks for all the blessings that he has bestowed on those of us who turn to him. We confide to him all that we think, all that we feel. We unburden our hearts. We tell him of our difficulties, our troubles, but also our joys and our gratitude.

Above all we admit that we are sinners, we implore his mercy, we ask him to heal us: "Only say the word, and I shall be healed." An unhealthy mind has as much need of healing as an unhealthy body, if not more so. "That, Lord, is what I have been, what I am now. Well, I come to you! My wretched states of mind that are in plain view, you see them as I see them..." reflected William of St Thierry[1] in his Golden Epistle.

---

1. Guillaume de Saint-Thierry, c. 1085-1148: a Benedictine monk who became a Cistercian, under the influence of his friend St Bernard of Clairvaux.

A matter of trust

Let us therefore ask the Lord to forgive us our faults, to heal us of all the ills caused by sin. The sinner who has complete faith in God, who commits himself/herself to him, who knows that he is Love in all its fullness, whose wayward nature does not prevent the truth from coming out: "In you Lord have I put my whole trust; I say: 'You are my God'. All my days are in your hand"[1] then that sinner may be sure that he or she has been redeemed by Christ, Saviour of the world.

It is none the less clear to us as the years go by that, as we take stock of our weak points and our shortcomings, we find in ourselves many traits of character that can be much improved. But there will always remain genetic traits that can never be effaced. The power of faith provides the ability to draw a distinction between the two on the authority of Christ's teachings, by relying on him alone and by acquiring an infinitesimal portion of his eternal wisdom that guides and leads us, that disposes all things, that gives a direction to our lives.

What is prayer?

Prayer consists in remaining quietly before God "in whom we sense the love he bears us". The quotation is from St Teresa of Avila, the 'great

1. Psalm 30(31):16,17.

Teresa'. This tranquil trust in the love which God has for us will progress through the test of his apparent silence in spite of our troubles and tribulations. It is on this pathway that we shall learn to give up all selfishness, to "minimise the me", and to pin all our hopes on the God of mercy who simply asks us to keep company with him. It is only by praying that we can be sure to remain with him in the perfect peace that he gives us, thus allowing him to occupy our consciousness in the way he chooses and at all times.

The way to find God

It is therefore in silence that God will speak to our hearts. There is never any reason to be troubled by this silence for its effect is precisely to draw us to him through prayer. It is even at the heart of our own silence that the Eternal Word is born. It is here that, in stillness and humility, we can detect an aura of divine grace for it is the place of God.

This action within us can be assimilated to the intimate nature of passive contemplation that is defined by St John of the Cross as "a secret communication... infused into the soul by the Holy Spirit in a way it knows not" (*The Dark Night of the Soul,* II, 17). This communication can only take place in the depth and pureness of faith "which is a dark night...: the more it darkens the soul and the more it imparts its own brightness to it" (St John of the Cross: *The Ascent of Mount Carmel,* 11,2). Here lies the whole mystery of the life of the Word of God within us.

In his *Life of St Benedict*, Meister Eckhart writes in the same vein: "In a deep silence, in which there is no longer anything that speaks to the soul, it is there and then that the Word is spoken in our reason." This way of finding God by prayer, this mode of humble access to his presence, is what Saint Matthew calls the "narrow gate... that leads to life" (Mt 7:13).

Faith deeper than speech

When praying, it is therefore not enough to talk to the Lord. We must get used to listening to him in the inmost depths of the soul without expecting the silence to be broken by the Lord in created words. We have to jump with our eyes closed into what John of the Cross calls the "abyss of pure faith". Dom Augustin Guillerand tells us that these moments of pure faith "...are momentous occasions... Faith, which has taken the name of trust, then takes root at depths which prepare wonderful states of heart-expansion" (Spiritual Writings, 1,58).

A loving gaze

The plan that we must adopt is to adhere to the Son of God, in all things, in all places, and at all times. Because he dominates everything by his love, he infuses harmony into everything. But if faith has failed to attain the purity and intensity which generate singleness of purpose and simplicity, then it may lead to another form of suffering, namely that of disappointment and frustration accompanied by internal tension or stress. We have not plucked up the necessary courage to commit ourselves. We are missing the harmony of Christ. We are getting the painful impression of having failed to keep our appointment with him. Prayer has become an apparent failure.

But a simple loving gaze or thought can alter everything. Any true act or sign of love is accompanied – to use the expression of Dom Le Masson – by a "leaping-out of the spirit" towards God or towards his Son. A lingering look charged with love is silence. Prayer itself then becomes only a silence of God, the very silence that God infuses into the soul by flooding it with his presence. Dom Le Masson has also said: "Souls that God completely occupies have nothing to say since their interior gaze says all and contains all that they would like to say" (Dom Le Masson: *Views*).

Under the influence of love, the soul can therefore only remain still, listening attentively. This silence becomes divine plenitude, the acme of grace, resting of the soul in God, the gate of the kingdom of heaven, and "the deliverance of the righteous from all their afflictions" (Ps 33[34]).

Can our Father be absent?

The "silence of God" has already been considered in the previous chapter. But another frequent subject of discussion today is the "absence" of God. Even believers who have deep faith are liable to be assailed by doubts. They may sometimes have the impression that their prayers are futile, that they are engaged in a monologue. And even the psalmist asks: "Where now is your God?" (Ps 41[42]: 3,12). Can it really be that he is "not available"? We are overcome by a feeling of doubt, uncertainty and loss.

The first observation that must be made here is that we only feel the absence of someone whom we know well, particularly if that 'someone' is loved and missed, whereas the Father of us all is really present and listening to what we have to say. Above all, what *appears* to us to be the absence of God is in reality our own absence. Let us therefore be honest with ourselves and acknowledge the truth in simple terms, as I propose to do in my turn: "I know, Lord, that you are never absent. Should I sometimes have the sad feeling that you have abandoned me, it is because I have paid no heed to your presence and I am the one to have moved away from you. I have got lost in my thoughts and my distractions and you have no longer occupied my mind. I ask your forgiveness, Lord, for having believed for a single moment that you were no longer with me, whereas I was in fact no longer with *you*."

Consenting to the presence of God

Let us therefore remain before the Lord in an attitude of receptiveness, patience, simplicity and humility which is not lowering but elevation of the soul in a state of total dependence. In order to become really true to ourselves, we feel a deep need for intimate communion which prefigures union with God, knowing that we conform to our identity and destiny only in him and through him. By living in an intimate personal relationship with our Creator, we discover both the reality and the truth of our existence. Our freewill offering of love can be expected to give rise to a revelation of self. But it is first necessary to turn away from our own will in order to be able to recognise and acclaim a Presence which existed before the creation of the world. Fervent prayer makes us conscious of the indwelling Spirit of God.

In order to welcome God in our hearts, we must drive out all vanity from our thoughts. We must become conscious of the nothingness of human greatness, of the relativity of man in the vastness of space. Destitute and masters of nothing, we are powerless against the ravages of time and the upheavals of the world. We are nothing more than frail, ephemeral creatures that await their end: an end that is eternity for the faithful few.

In our weakness and emptiness, we must be ready to receive everything from God in a communion of love, which is the basic principle and the ultimate objective of our brief passage on earth. As we are reminded and encouraged by the well-known paradox of St Paul, it is in fact our great weakness that gives us strength and makes life meaningful.

The presence of God in the world through Jesus Christ

How is it possible to read or hear the Word of God without believing in Love ineffable that enfolds us? Can Love have the name of Unknowable? Does the Word not announce the Name of Love? What is that voice that we hear in our hearts? It calls us to pledge our whole being and to put our whole hope in Love that is neither unknowable nor inaccessible. It is the voice of God in our Lord Jesus Christ whom we see acting and speaking through the Gospel, whom we meet in person, whom we welcome with joy and gladness, and whom we receive in our intimacy each time we take part in the Holy Eucharist. The Son of God has told us in these very words: "Anyone who has seen me has seen the Father" (Jn 14:9).

In Jesus Christ, God is present to the whole of humanity. In our prayer, our role is to remain in this presence in a state of full awareness of our spiritual poverty, to offer our desire to let him take control in all things, especially in any distressing situation. Let us rest assured that we are never alone since Christ lives in us. When we pray for ourselves, for those who are closely related to us, for all men and women, living or dead; when we pray with the psalms, the Bible or the liturgy; it is the personal voice of Christ, the voice of his Church also, that rises up from our hearts.

A remedy for everything in Christ

Prayer, meditation, petition, intercession... Our cause is heard in advance: "Anything you ask in my name I will do", Jesus has promised us, "so that the Father may be glorified in the Son" (Jn 14:13). And even if we have the impression that we don't know how to pray, if we can do no more than utter a few faltering words, Jesus can be depended on to interpret what we are trying to say and to come to our aid. The Holy Spirit also has a part to play, and we shall return to this later. But by turning to our Saviour with love, even while remaining silent, we shall always find a remedy for our deficiencies, for our momentary difficulties which are then reduced to their true proportions.

Let us make no mistake: we are never capable of seeing things and human beings as Christ sees them. Let us therefore always be wary of value judgements that we may make about others, of hasty conclusions inspired by anxiety, by jealousy, or by anything that we consider as an injustice towards us. Let us trust, on the contrary, in the wisdom of Christ with absolute confidence in a spirit of absolute humility. It is in his light that we shall learn to accept people, to adapt to new situations, surroundings and events.

Utter commitment to the Father

"Jesus has told me to turn to you, Father, and to trust in your guidance. I let you take over. I let you manage everything your way. I agree to all that you want to make of me, all that I am even no longer conscious of desiring. Let my last words be those uttered by Jesus on the Cross: 'Into your hands I commit my spirit.'"

Commitment into the Lord's hands, or self-abandonment, can only be experienced in the simplicity and detachment that are the natural products of confidence and peace of mind.

To believe is to count on the Lord's help

To believe in the untiring love of Christ, of the Blessed Virgin Mary, of all the saints such as St Benedict or St Anne, of all the servants of the Lord who have left us in the hope of eternal life, is to show an unfailing attitude of openness and welcome in our hearts to those who are watching over us as we well know, even if we perceive no outward and visible sign of their presence. To believe is to show gentleness and interest in each person we meet for we can recognise the face of Jesus or of Mary in that person. To believe is to identify ourselves with "those who know their need of God", those mentioned first by Jesus in the Beatitudes, those who have learned from their moral or material hardships to count solely on the help of the Lord, for he is "close to the broken-hearted." By reading and re-reading Psalm 33[34], we shall draw solace and relief from the psalmist's words of comfort.

No defeat for those who are one with Christ

"Look towards him and be radiant" (Ps 33[34]:5). The English saint and martyr, John Fisher, recited this phrase when he saw that the sun was shining behind the scaffold. The psalm from which it was taken is sometimes known as the hymn of martyrs for the Lord sets them free from all their terrors. This is above all a hymn for all those who have to endure the little torments of their everyday lives. They may feel discouraged by their failure to overcome past trials, their weakness at the present time, or their secret fear that they will be unable to continue to bear up under the strain of suffering. But they may remain quite certain that there will be no defeat for all those who are one with the Paschal Lamb on the Cross.

A secret language that speaks of hope

The Lord is our one hope. "We rejoice in our hope of sharing the glory of God" (Rom 5:2). Steadfast hope is an abiding reality, like faith and love. If we give up all hope, the other two will suffer. But if we are full of hope, we can only increase in faith and in love, to the great benefit of those around us. Hope is the light of our life that no dark shadow of failing confidence or doubt must ever be allowed to obscure.

The secret language of our life and our prayer finds its expression in confidence and praise. Everything in the life of this world has something to tell us of the love and the glory of God, of suffering that is only transient, of the happiness that will be the final and permanent state of the faithful believer. God reveals himself through an inner call that finds an echo in an ardent impulse of the heart: "O Lord, open my lips and my mouth shall proclaim your praise" (Ps 50[51]:15).

In our secret dialogue with God, we too often fail to submit ourselves in complete devotion to him, lacking in attention and therefore in understanding. To engage in a dialogue while praying is to accept abandonment and docility, to make all our thoughts responsive to God, to revive our faith, thus radiating a force which opens our existence beyond ourselves. This vital force is nourished by God's promise to Abraham: "I shall bless you and multiply your descendants... because you have obeyed my voice" (Gen 22:17,18).

Presence of God. Hope in God. Hope is the "anchor of the soul" that gives a sure hold on life, that generates courage and strength, opening our hearts and minds to the grace and peace already offered by the coming of Christ.

In hope we rejoice in the presence of God's infinite love and faithfulness. This is our ultimate reason for persevering in the faith until the end of our earthly course. It is even the whole meaning of life in this world of exile.

The foundation of prayer

Why do we exist? Our existence is a gift of love and grace. Our first act of faith consists in granting our unreserved acceptance, in giving our full consent to God's creative and redemptive project, to his continual and permanent presence in what is conventionally termed the 'heart', that is to say the inmost feelings and deep awareness that exist in every individual.

Awareness and assent form the basis of prayer. Prayer may therefore be defined as the awareness of our fundamental need for the boundless love that God has towards us all.

When we live our faith in prayer, we live it knowingly in the presence of the God of the living and in the presence of all our fellow human beings, living or dead. When we turn our thoughts to them, our minds will accordingly be imbued with this knowledge, thus conditioning our behaviour towards our neighbours.

Welcoming of the Word leads to joy

We all tend towards our Creator through Jesus Christ whose word we welcome in the "communion of saints" or, more explicitly, the union of all believers in the same faith, in heaven and on earth. May all that is living within us respond to this word and we shall experience an unspeakable and indefinable inner joy that we would never wish to exchange for any other. To respond to this word, to the Word of God which is our Lord Jesus Christ, is the essence of prayer. When we pray, our ardent aspiration becomes a veritable adherence that involves our entire being in a devoted, submissive and silent state of expectancy.

Jesus Christ, our true reason for living

We know that Christ is always with us, that his presence ensures the continuity and the constancy of our prayer, that our relationship with him exists within our inmost selves and that, through him, we put our trust in the love of God which is bestowed upon each one of us personally as someone unique. We have to believe this, to be faithful and constant, and to follow the example of

St John, "the disciple whom Jesus loved", by resting our heads on the breast of the Divine Master who is our hope and our whole reason for living. We feel the need for his presence and nothing else.

A silence that is the fullness of love

As we pray in the presence of Christ, we are blessed and inspired by the exemplary silence of the Father. We must in our turn strive to keep silence in his sight. This is a dominant silence taken back from God, a silence of welcome and contemplation filled with the plenitude of love, the promise of a celestial future in which all is grace and gladness, an infinite hereafter, so remote and yet so near that it is already within us.

Why have doubts about the gift of God?

At times of darkness, of "wandering in the wilderness", of the "dryness" experienced by St Thérèse of Lisieux, it may happen that, in spite of our faith, we have doubts about the true nature of our lives deep down within us. But human life is not self-sustaining; it has been given to us by our Creator. To be doubtful about the gift of God, the source of all love, even at the darkest and most difficult moments of our existence, would be to cease from believing that we are children of God. If the father of a family is able to provide his children with the food they require, then in that case, says St Luke, "...how much more will the

Heavenly Father give the Holy Spirit to those (of his children) who ask him!" (Lk 11:13). We therefore have to live in prayer as in life itself, with assurance and deep abiding conviction.

Praying in the sight of God

> Search me out, O God, and know my heart;
> put me to the proof and know my thoughts.
>
> *Psalm 138[139]:23*

In the sight of God, we pray in abandonment to him and to his purpose for us, fully conscious of the constant indwelling of his Presence, and of the greatness of God that is our strength:

"God is greater than our conscience and discerns everything" (1 Jn 3:20).

Beginning with this phrase from the Letter of St John, Dom Lefebvre proposes a few guidelines in his book *The Silence of Prayer* and helps us to understand what the Lord expects us to do:

"To perceive in the depths of our faith in him what it is to exist in his sight.

To step beyond our obscurities and allow ourselves to be searched by this penetrating look that sees what remains hidden from our view.

A look that allows perception of a beyond surpassing all that we call love.

To be simply open to him. Offered.

The emptiness of our poverty can no longer be simply emptiness and poverty, in this look that recreates us in his image.

To let him dispel all our shadows.

As he looks at us, to see ourselves as we really are, to discover the real truth about ourselves.

As he looks at us, to perceive what becomes of humility that allows full access to love."

Simplicity and consolation of prayer

Access to love – to use the words just cited – begins by welcoming Christ with open arms and saying with St Paul: "*Marana tha*". This first-century Aramaic expression which appears in the *Didache*, a book of liturgical teachings used in the primitive Christian Church, is a prayer meaning simply: "Come, O Lord". It is an appeal that comes directly from the very bottom of the heart: "Come, Lord Jesus. Come to my aid. You are all I have. I count on you for you are my Saviour. I give thanks to you, Lord, for your great glory."

Said with sincerity, these very simple words take us far beyond the stage of mere asking or supplication. They are basically a declaration of love and hope in full consciousness of the grace that is received from our Lord. Let us allow ourselves to be penetrated by this grace and we shall reach new depths of faith. We shall then see, by the light of the love of Christ, that prayer is pure simplicity and solace to the soul. Prayer is simple and reassuring when we reflect that Jesus Christ always prays in us through the Holy Spirit. We receive prayer from him. Prayer is communion with Christ. Prayer is thanksgiving. This is the whole point and meaning of the Eucharist.

The simplicity of prayer is the yardstick that

serves to measure our faith in the greatness and simplicity of a Saviour who comes to dwell in the deep intimacy of welcoming hearts and knows us far better than we know ourselves.

A call that is always heard

All those who are familiar with suffering and distress must realise that they can never be abandoned or left to themselves in a state of utter helplessness if they turn resolutely to the Lord and appeal to him. An appeal which rests on faith and implicit trust will always be heard, however poor the terms in which it is expressed. As St James said: "The prayer offered in faith will save the sick man and the Lord will raise him from his bed" (Jas 5:15).

Jesus himself observed in reply to Martha: "One thing alone is necessary" (Lk 10:42). We are to understand from this that the Word comes before all worldly considerations. As we remain before God in prayer, we must strive to give him our undivided attention without expecting anything in return. God invites us to listen to the Word (*Logos*) which is Christ, to store it preciously in our memory so that we may find in it an unending source of heavenly peace and relief.

Unconditional faith and assiduous commitment will allow us to stay in God's company and to know with certainty that he has "the power to do immeasurably more for us than all we can ask or even conceive" (Eph 3:20).

From darkness to light with the Good Shepherd

Prayer filled with hope, confidence, gratitude, at the beginning or at the end of days full of activities and preoccupations in which obstacles are never lacking: the course of life continues inexorably, day by day, but is often crossed by shadows, for troubles neither cease nor choose. At the end of this course is the light that never fails. The source of this light can already be perceived when we have at last understood that a protecting hand is always guarding us and guiding us infallibly, untiringly, just as the Good Shepherd guards and guides his sheep. The human sheep that we are love him, follow him and remain faithful to him. And yet we often have the feeling that we have not always answered his call and have strayed from his ways...

God beckons us to return to him

When night has fallen and we meditate in the silence of introspection, when we go over in our minds all that has been said or done during the day, we recall the lapses that have led us astray, filling Love with sadness. But God always beckons us to return to him in a spirit of contrition and thanksgiving. He invites us to entrust our daily lives and even our entire existence to his tender mercy. We need no longer hesitate to put ourselves in his hands and cling to him with utter reliance. We may then cast aside all the worldly worries that have been encumbering our minds, and ask him to forgive our wanderings from the straight path as we pray: "Lord, have mercy upon us, forgive us our sins, and bring us to everlasting life."

The Jesus Prayer

The habit of turning to God through our Lord and Saviour Jesus Christ and through the Holy Spirit can be built-up by means of the "Jesus Prayer". In that little masterpiece of spiritual literature known as *The Way of a Pilgrim*, a Russian pilgrim of unknown name (believed to have been a monk of Mount Athos) relates how he acquired the habit of repeating all day long during his long peregrinations: "Lord Jesus Christ, have mercy on me."

Already in the fifth century, this prayer was constantly being recited in Eastern monasteries. But in the sixth century, St John Climacus, a monk of Mount Sinai (and Abbot of St Catherine's monastery), made one of the first allusions to the 'Jesus Prayer' in his 'Ladder of Paradise' in which he gave the following advice: "Let the remembrance of Jesus be present in every breath you draw, and then you will know the value of divine quietness."[1]

Let us therefore follow this fine example of a secular practice which complies with St Paul's exhortation to the Thessalonians: "Pray without ceasing."

---

1. Another translation reads: "...you will know the fruit of silence and solitude."

The intellectual and spiritual activity of any Christian can never achieve fulfilment without constantly reflecting upon the life of Jesus, without studying and practising his teachings, without constantly repeating his holy name. The mind must be untiringly directed towards Christ. It is therefore this prayer in particular that can be recited at any moment and in all circumstances: "Lord Jesus Christ, Son of the living God, have mercy on me, a sinner; have mercy on us all." This is the prototype of all prayer, together with the "Our Father..."

To love as Jesus loved

St John Climacus also stated: "God grants the gift of prayer to those who pray." It is by praying that one learns to pray, just as it is by walking that children learn to walk. Our whole lives should be prayerful, or in other words conscious of God's presence. But we must remain content with the prayer that is given to us. "Let us be assured," says St Benedict in his Holy Rule, "that it is not in saying a great deal that we shall be heard, but in purity of heart" (R.B.20).

To use the first person as each one of us would do, this is what we might say: "It matters little what words I use provided that I consciously remain in the sight of my Father, that I allow myself to be pervaded by his Holy Spirit, that I love as Jesus loved, that I devote my life entirely to prayer and to the necessity of love. Have I not found in the recognition of this necessity the pathway that leads me to discover the deep truth of my being?

Has it not taught me to accept myself as a free gift of grace, the fruit of love, and to regard all God's creatures, every human being, as a beautiful miracle? Isn't this the true condition of contemplation? Faith enables me to understand that the Creator dwells in my soul and fills me with intimate knowledge of his presence within me. In fact, everything in my existence becomes contemplation and prayer, in which love of my neighbour and compassion play a leading part. It is only on this pathway that I am capable of meeting all my commitments in life with a new outlook and a heart transformed by the Holy Spirit."

Contemplative prayer, which is a mystical communion charged with love, pulls us away from ourselves in order to displace and re-centre us upon the Kingdom of God. Thus it is a loving call to the Father, to the Son, and to the Holy Spirit.

The role of the Virgin Mary and of the saints

As she listens to our humble prayer of entreaty: "Holy Mary, Mother of God, pray for us sinners", the Blessed Virgin Mary makes it clear to us that, as the mother of Jesus Christ our Lord and our God, she is the heavenly mother of the children of God. She therefore intercedes for all those who turn to her for a mother's comfort. It is hardly surprising that, in the secular life and literature of the West, the Virgin Mary has always symbolised the nobility of woman and that all generations have indeed called her blessed (cf. Lk 1:48).

Still accompanied by St Joseph and by her parents, St Joachim and St Anne, the mother of God watches over us at all times with unfailing compassion and tenderness. Her primary intention is always to give herself entirely to God. She continues to acknowledge the grace she receives by singing of the wonders performed through her by the Almighty. But at all times, she is ready on the spur of the moment to dismiss all thoughts of herself from her mind in order to consider the plan that God is carrying out in the world of today. In his work of salvation for us all, she is called upon by grace to play a key role.

Another object of prayer in the eyes of many believers is to honour and contemplate with deep devotion all those eminent witnesses who have responded to the love of God by leading exemplary lives at the cost of self-sacrifice and in the service of charity. This 'cloud of witnesses' includes the saints whom we hold in special veneration and who are efficacious in their intercession for us.

"Sanctified in Christ Jesus and called to be saints" (1 Cor 1:2), these saints of God bear the flaming torch that illuminates our hearts with its heavenly light, guiding us[1] and exercising the power of salvation in a spirit of kindness and concern. All

---

1. As St Anne guided Yvon Nicolazic to her buried statue in one of her many apparitions, after asking him to rebuild her church in accordance with the will of God. Today the shrine of St Anne near Auray in Brittany, visited by Pope John Paul II in 1996, attracts pilgrims and visitors from all parts of the world.

of them ask for one thing alone: to guide us to the eternal happiness that they will share with us.

Praying "in the name of Jesus Christ"

A Christian's prayer is above all Christ's prayer that we make our own. The role of those who pray does not consist in finding formulas but in being readily receptive to the word of Christ who is always with us and within us in order to intercede with the Father on our behalf. All Christian prayers are therefore prayers "in the name of Jesus Christ our Lord", that is to say, in Christ and with him. According to the Gospel of St John, Jesus himself refers to this subject no less than four times, which shows us the importance he attaches to it: "In very truth I tell you, if you ask the Father for anything in my name, he will give it to you. So far you have asked nothing in my name. Ask and you will receive, that your joy may be complete" (Jn 16:23-24).

We too, are children of God

While imitating Christ at prayer, we must never imagine that our prayers are heard with 'half an ear' by a God who is impersonal and distant. Like God the Son, he is even much closer to us than we are to ourselves. Let us bear in mind that our prayer is always a word to the Father who has revealed himself in Jesus Christ. Jesus himself spoke to the Father just as a child would have done, with the same intimate simplicity, the same trusting submission. He has always called God *"Abba"*, a term of affection meaning Father (more precisely: Daddy, or Dad). And Jesus has given us the right to pronounce it with him since we, too, are children of God.

As St Paul reminds us, the Holy Spirit joins with our spirit in testifying that we are children and therefore heirs: "We are God's heirs and Christ's fellow heirs, if we share his sufferings now in order to share his splendour hereafter." He then adds these encouraging words: "The sufferings of the present time are not worthy to be compared with the glory which shall be revealed in us" (Rom 8:16-18).

Further on in the same chapter, St Paul talks about prayer: "In the same way the Spirit helps us in our weakness; for we do not know how to pray as we ought, but the Spirit himself intercedes for us with sighs too deep for words" (Rom 8:26).

Making ourselves as small as little children

We therefore only need to express ourselves in prayer with submissiveness to the Spirit but with assurance even if, in our adult eyes, our prayer seems to be short, commonplace, over-simple or childlike. For it is a fact that our 'mind's eye' is incapable of discerning the plenitude of Love and has only a dim perception of the truth. Let us therefore accept to live our helplessness in prayer by making ourselves as small as little children.

In the spiritual sense, the 'little ones' are the humble disciples of all ages to whom the mystery of the kingdom of heaven is revealed, who are enlightened by their reverent and obedient fear of the Lord, and who glorify his holy name without attributing any glory to themselves. As St Benedict himself says in the Prologue of his Rule: "It is they who, fearing the Lord, do not pride themselves on their good observance but are convinced that the good which is in them comes from God and not from themselves..."

In the eyes of the Lord, a 'little one' is any one of those who, while remaining fully conscious of the Lord's infinite and eternal love, attach no importance to themselves and have no sense of ownership in anything they may think or do. They are without pretension and devoid of pride: "For everyone who exalts himself will be humbled; and whosoever humbles himself will be exalted" (Lk 14:11). To be little is both an art and a state. The secret is to be content with what little there is and to remain simple, without intellectualism or activism which is often little more than a personal quest for self-satisfaction. Far from being pejorative, littleness in this context is the quality of character and of life of the man who bows his head, saying like the publican (tax-gatherer) of the Gospel: "Lord, you know that I am a sinner. I am not worthy to raise my eyes to heaven" (cf. Lk 18). But it is the same person who is always ready to listen, who is gentle and tolerant, who spends his or her life seeking peace in order to bring to others at least a small measure of serenity and contentment.

Jesus himself has declared clearly and unambiguously: "Unless you are converted and become as little children, you will never enter the kingdom of Heaven" (Mt 18:3,4).

We are reminded here of these beautiful verses of Psalm 130[131]:

> O Lord, my heart is not proud
> nor are my eyes haughty.
>
> I do not busy myself in great matters
> or in things too wonderful for me.
>
> But I have calmed and quieted my soul
> like a weaned child upon its mother's breast.
>
> Like a child on its mother's breast
> is my soul within me.

Union of the soul with God

It is in the fullness of simplicity that the souls of the small adoptive children of God that we are can enter into communion with him. The soul is simplified in the peace and unity of silence. Silence and peace of the soul cannot exist without each other. The silence of contemplation leads to peace that is not of this world, the "peace of God which passes all understanding" (Phil 4:7). Inner silence that attains to divine tranquillity is the *hesychia* of the Eastern Church. This Greek term refers to a state of mind that fosters unity and deep spiritual peace, thus permitting contemplation of God's glory in the person of Jesus Christ. *Hesychia* empties the soul of all outside influence, of concern over its own states, of any desire which is not for the glory of God: *vacate et videte quoniam ego sum Deus* – learn to be empty of all things (within and without) and you will see that I am God. This injunction is taken from Psalm 45(46) which says to all men: "Be still and know that I am God." In different terms: "Lay down your arms, seek peace and withdraw." This is the relinquishment and detachment of the Far East philosophy of Zen. We abandon ourselves to God who acts in us, for us and through us. This abdication of self, this death of self, this *nada* of St John of the Cross, is an act of commitment of our spirit into the Lord's hands. The soul is then transformed by pureness and love which are total self-denial and perfect resignation. It is in this way that union with God can finally be accomplished.

The last place

We should be quite wrong to feel discouraged, no matter what weakness, deficiency or poverty of mind we may suffer from. Even if we remain convinced that we are utterly unworthy and incompetent, we have nothing to fear and everything to gain by persisting in prayer. It is not intellectual ability or knowledge that brings us closer to God, but love alone.

Should we be lacking in courage or inspiration, should the right words fail to come, making us feel incapable of expressing ourselves freely and clearly, we must be content to keep quiet, knowing that silent contemplation leads to harmony with Christ.

It may be concluded that speech is not essential to prayer. Indeed Our Lord does not expect us to make a speech to him. Since he already knows us to the inmost depths of our being, he also knows exactly what is essential for our needs. He simply asks us to confirm our faith and to accept the last place among men, for it is the first in the heart of God the Father.

Divine grace

If we are self-effacing before the Lord in an act of humility and deep faith in the immense mystery of Love in which we are enwrapped, he will then come forward and reach out to support us and comfort us.

If effacement is neither withdrawal nor obliteration of self but, on the contrary, lucid acceptance and trust without artifice, then prayer becomes openness and wonderment.

If we persevere in an attitude of vigilance and rapt attention, if we adore the Lord with fervour and our heart goes straight out to him, then the divine grace will calm all agitation and will spread deep down within us.

Overcome by mounting thrills of incomparable sweetness, the body will feel this strong current of divine love which brings a free pardon for all our faults, fills us with heavenly bliss, dispels all sadness and infuses new life, thus producing a sense of well-being and renewed strength which combine to relieve the intolerable burden of affliction, suffering and distress.

It is in such moments of special privilege that we shall truly be able to affirm with the psalmist: "The unfailing love of the Lord enfolds those who trust in him" (Ps 31[32]:10).